To My Readers

Be sure to write to me at jimhewittwriting@aol.com. When I receive your e-mail, I will add you to my SPECIAL e-mail list. This group of readers will receive updates on any already published subject matter. Also, any time I publish a new book they will know about it in advance.

“Be Just and Fear Not”

ISBN: 978-1-4303-0820-1

Published by Lulu Distribution (www.lulu.com)

Printed in the USA.

Snow

Come look at me,

I am a beautiful sight.

In one storm,

the world appears white.

When all the hills are covered,

I am the brightest around.

When I melt,

all my splendor is gone.

I hope that you may see,

all my beauty,

because, breathe and I vanish instantly.

Jim Hewitt (1983)

Other Titles by James Hewitt

Sick Building Syndrome – 2006

Did you know that the Environmental Protection Agency (EPA) has in the past, defined indoor air pollution as one of the most significant environmental threats to human health? In 1994, the Occupational Safety and Health Administration (OSHA) proposed a set of indoor air quality standards.

The causes of how a building can be considered "sick" will be explained and discussed. The prevention and some solutions for the syndrome, known as SBS, will be discussed. The ventilation issues that promote SBS will be broached. Some ways to help prevent or fix SBS will also be explained. I will review methods for the prevention of SBS and offer some solutions to help your building become a healthier place. This will benefit you and all the people who work, live, or play in the building. In the last chapter, I will explain in detail about my plan for the creation of a Team to monitor your building and any complaints regarding SBS.

The Christmas Tree

James P. Hewitt, RN

In Memory Of

This book is written for and dedicated to all the children worldwide who have never had the pleasure or opportunity to enjoy a Christmas celebration.

Christmas traditionally is supposed to be about faith, family, love, food, gifts, and should be, in general, a fun time. This book has been written to honor children everywhere. I am going to donate the majority of the money earned from every book sold, to reputable organizations that help needy children.

As a young adult, I remember my father once saying, “Children are the true innocents of the world”. Looking back at my life, I realize that my father had hardly been ever wrong. He loved being around children. He told me that hate, fear, aggression, and lying were all learned behaviors by children from their dealings with adults.

The Holiday Seasons are for children of all ages and sizes. Yes, even you, the Senior Citizen who is not physically a child. You can still feel like a child in your mind and heart. What better joy is there than the one felt while giving and receiving presents? My hope is that by writing this book I can help children.

I am going to ask you to think back to your first memory of Christmas. It probably includes a memory of a decorated and brightly lit tree surrounded by colorfully wrapped presents. A smile can always be seen on even the most selfish and bitter person when viewing a well-designed Christmas tree.

Thanks

For my mother, Rose Ann Hewitt, who has always been my number ONE supporter. No matter what the circumstances, she has always believed in me. As a child, I often made life a challenge. I can account for almost every gray hair that she now has. It is true what they say about a mothers' love, "It never ends."

In loving memory of my father, John Alfred Hewitt, who always taught me to never take "No" for an answer. To always follow my beliefs, constantly strive to do my best, and always "keep the faith".

A special thanks to my wife, Virginia Anne Hewitt for all her extra support. Thanks for being patient with all my long hours of research. Without her support, none of my books would have been possible. She is definitely my better half. She is my light in the darkness.

Love; Just a Four-Letter Word?

Love, is it like a drop of morning dew,
lasting briefly until the morning sun
Or is it like a droplet of rain,
starting in the heavens slowly working to the sea.

Love, is it powerful as the summer storms,
arriving instantly, but not enduring.
Can it be great as a mountain,
always there and everlasting.

Love, might it be like an eagle,
fierce and strong.
Is it simply like the butterfly,
radiant and cherished.

To each, Love has its own meaning,
but when you find it, you will know,
and you will never let it go.

Jim Hewitt (May 1995)

Table of Contents

Introduction

First of all, I want to thank you for purchasing this book. I hope that it helps to expand your knowledge regarding the Christmas tree and that you find it a rewarding read.

This creation of this book was purely by chance. A group of my co-workers were discussing Christmas and why decorations, trees, and other customs are practiced. Have you ever wondered the same? One question was regarding the Christmas tree. Where did the idea originate? Who might be responsible for the tradition? Was a person responsible for the tree or was it a cultural phenomena that grew. All these thoughts and questions caused me to conduct a little research.

I wrote this book to inform anyone who might ever wonder the same thing. Think back to your first memory of Christmas. Most likely, it probably includes a memory of a decorated and brightly lit tree. A smile can always be seen on even the most selfish and bitter person when viewing a well designed Christmas tree.

Throughout history, trees have played an important part in many winter religious celebrations. For many centuries, many pagan festivals and celebrations utilized trees when honoring their gods and spirits. The Vikings considered the evergreen to be a powerful symbol. The evergreen was a reminder to the Vikings that the darkness and cold of the winter season would eventually end. The tree also reminded them that the green of spring would always return. The Ancient Druids of England, France, and Ireland decorated oak trees with fruit and candles to honor their gods of the harvest. At the festival "Saturnalia" the Romans decorated trees with trinkets and candles. There have been many legends surrounding the use of the Christmas tree. In this book, I hope to educate the reader about the trees of Pre-Christianity History, Christianity History, the Evolution of the tree, and review the most common types of trees used at Christmas. I will also discuss real vs. fake Christmas trees, the care of a real tree, and general household Christmas tree safety.

Remember as you read this book to keep an open mind. This book has been written as an informative piece of literature. The facts in this book are not intended to violate or upset any one person's religious beliefs. I have tried to be as objective and factual as much as possible.

So, why do we have a decorated Christmas tree? Think you already know. As you read this book, I am willing to bet that you will learn a lot about this Christmas symbol.

I have also included in this book some information regarding the evolution of the tree. Also, I will describe the most common types of trees used. I have included a chapter discussing the real vs. the fake Christmas tree. The Wreath and other goodies are also mentioned. As a Registered Nurse, it would be irresponsible of me if I did not discuss real tree care and holiday safety. Please read on and find out how much you think you truly know. I am positive that every person who reads this book will learn something new.

Chapter One – Pre-Christian History

To understand about the significance of a tree for worship, I first need to delve into a little history. The Egyptians were part of a long line of cultures that worshipped the evergreen. The Egyptians would often bring green Date palm leaves into their homes to symbolize life's triumph over death, during the Winter Solstice.

The Christmas tree originated in Northern Europe from the pre-Christian Pagan cultures. The tree has an extensive history and has become a common sight during the winter season in numerous cultures throughout the world. Throughout history, the origins of the Christmas tree are often explained as a Christian-ization of an ancient Pagan idea. For the Pagans, the evergreen tree as a symbol represented the celebration of the renewal of life.

At this point you may be asking yourself, "What is a Pagan?" The Indiana University Pagan web site defines Paganism as, "a religion, or perhaps a set of various spiritual paths and traditions, that celebrates reverence for the Earth and all its creatures. This question is actually quite complex since every follower of an earth-based spiritual tradition would probably give you a different definition. Fortunately, there are several concepts that seem to be quite popular among most of us. "Pagans" generally believe that all life is interconnected and try to experience this interconnectivity as part of their religious practices. In short, Pagans believe in more than one God.

Their primary God, unlike in Christianity, is a female who is symbolized as the Mother Earth. The Pagans also believe in a male God. The male God is believed to be the heavens that surround and protect the Mother Earth. Still the Mother Earth is the primary God.

The decoration of the Christmas tree, decking the halls with boughs of holly, and even the kiss provoking mistletoe all seem so natural to us now during the holiday season, just as it would have felt to the Pagans throughout history. Let us get beyond the commercialization of Christmas. Think about the symbolism and the psychology behind it.

Evergreen trees and the clippings of evergreen shrubs are widely harvested from the Northern landscape and brought inside to promote good cheer, friendship, love, and hope. Christmas trees remind us of better times yet to come. They also look great as decorations. The trees allow greenery into a drab dull season dominated by colors of white, gray, and brown. This season unfortunately has very little natural light and greenish colors.

The Roman Catholic Church decided in the fourth century that Christmas would be celebrated on December 25. This was due to the Pagan celebrations of the Roman Saturnalia, which was celebrated at the same time of the year. The traditions such as feasting and exchanging gifts carried over with the conversion of the Pagans to Christians. Other traditions were too controversial to carry over, such as using the clippings of evergreen shrubs from the landscape to decorate houses. This was a common practice during the December celebrations of Saturnalia, which was strictly forbidden by the Church.

Here are some examples throughout history of Pagans and their use of the tree in their religious celebrations. Patron trees, such as Thor's Oak and the figurative Yggdrasil held special significance for ancient Germanic tribes. For the early Germanic tribes the Yule tradition was celebrated by sacrificing male animals and slaves by suspending them from the branches of trees.

In Scandinavia, the Pagan kings in the past would sacrifice nine males of each species in the sacred groves every ninth year. Dionysus in his triumphant return is depicted standing behind God while holding an evergreen. The tree also reminded them that the green of spring would always return.

The Ancient Druids of England, France, and Ireland decorated oak trees with fruit and candles to honor their Gods of the harvest. At the festival “Saturnalia”, the Romans decorated trees with trinkets and candles. Roman mosaics from current day Tunisia, depict the mythic triumphant return from India of the Greek God of wine and male fertility, Dionysus. In these mosaics God is shown carrying a tapering coniferous tree.

In England, some Medieval legends concentrated on the miraculous "flowering" of trees at Christmas time. This legend still holds power over people. Even in modern times a branch of flowering Glastonbury thorn is still sent annually for the Queen's Christmas table in the United Kingdom.

The conversion of pre-Anglo Saxon Roman Britain is believed to have started with a hallucination. Constantine, a heathen warlord had this hallucination while on the eve of leading his troops into a great battle. He would later become a great Roman Emperor. He interpreted his hallucination as showing that Jesus Christ of Nazareth had become the universe's new supreme God of War. Years later while on his deathbed, Constantine was officially baptized as a Christian.

Thanks to Emperor Constantine's conversion in 312 AD, the Church was given unlimited power to tax, outlaw, regulate, and otherwise suppress competing religions. This was a power that was strongest in the bigger cities of that period of history. Unlike in the city, the country folk were unaffected by such coercion, which allowed the old religions to survive.

According to Wikipedia Encyclopedia, “The historical phenomenon of Christianization, the conversion of individuals to Christianity or the conversion of entire peoples at once, also includes the practice of converting Pagan practices, Pagan religious imagery, Pagan sites and the Pagan calendar to Christian uses. In Antiquity, Christianization was effected only partly through laws against sacrifice and sorcery and official conversions of temples to Christian churches. It was effected also by the degradation of Pagan Gods into daimones (demons) and the Christianization of existing rites. The Free Dictionary defines Christianization as “a change of religion; usually a conversion to the Catholic faith".

In many instances, the recycling of pre-Christian activities and beliefs was officially sanctioned by the Catholic Church. Pope Gregory the First, believed that the conversion of Pagans to Christianity would be easier if the people were allowed to retain the outward forms of their traditions. Often Pagan religious sites were torn down and a Church was built on the ruins of that site.

The Catholic Church designated their own religious holidays to coincide with all the major Pagan holidays. Here are some examples, All Saints Day and Samhain, Christmas and Yule Tide, Easter and Earth Day. The Church believed that people were used to certain days and sites for worship, so by adopting those sites and worship days it would help with Christianization of the Pagans. The Christmas tree is often explained as a Christianization of the ancient pagan idea. To Pagans the evergreen tree represents a celebration of the renewal of life.

The Pope, with the conversion of the Pagans, claimed that the traditions were now in honor of the Christian God. Here is a quote from a letter he wrote, "to the end that, whilst some gratifications are outwardly permitted them, they may the more easily consent to the inward consolations of the grace of God". It intended that the traditions and practices could still exist as long as the rationale for them was forgotten. The syncretism in Christian tradition has long been recognized by Modern day scholars. The Roman Catholic Church has even in recent times acknowledged the instances of syncretism of other non-Catholic religions.

Chapter Two - Christian History

The Gospels in the Bible describe the birth of Jesus in great detail. The Gospels never mention the date, so historians do not know the exact date. The Roman Catholic Church chose December 25th as the day to celebrate the birth of Jesus. By choosing that day, the Church replaced a Pagan festival that honored the birth of Mithra, who was the god of light. Historians cannot however, agree on the initial original use of the Christmas tree. There are many myths and stories of how the Christmas tree came to be used as a Christian symbol to help with the celebration of Jesus Christ's birthday. I will try to give as many of the stories to you. It is up to you to determine which one you like best.

In the 7th century, a monk named Boniface from Devonshire, England went to Germany to teach the Word of God. He did many good works in Germany. Today we know of him as St. Boniface. One story tells of Saint Boniface who came upon a group of Pagans who had gathered around an oak tree. They were preparing to sacrifice a child. The story tells of how the Saint flattened the oak tree with one blow of his fist to save the child's life. A small fir sprang up in its place, which Saint Boniface told the Pagans was the Tree of Life and represented the life of Christ.

Another version of this story tells how in Germany almost 1,000 years ago, St Boniface came across a group of Pagans worshipping at the base of an oak tree. In anger, St Boniface is said to have cut down the oak tree and much to his amazement a young fir tree sprung up from the roots of the oak tree.

Another legend has it that Boniface used the triangular shape of the Fir tree to describe the Holy Trinity of God the Father, his son Jesus Christ, and Holy Spirit. The converted people began to revere the Fir tree as God's Tree. They worshiped the fir tree as strongly as they had previously revered the Oak.

By the 12th century the Fir tree was being hung, upside down, from ceilings at Christmas in Central Europe, as a symbol of Christianity. St. Boniface took the tree as a sign of the Christian faith. St. Boniface appears to be at the center of most early stories regarding the origin of the fir tree, which is now known as the Christmas tree.

There are many written stories of when, who, and where the first Christmas tree was erected. I will include each story that I came upon during my research.

Historically, the first decorated tree was at Riga in Latvia, in 1510. An octagonal plaque hanging in the town square reads "The First New Year's Tree in Riga in 1510”. A monk, Martin Luther, in the early 16th century is said to have decorated a small Christmas tree with candles. This was to show children how the stars twinkled through the dark night of the winter season. There is another version of this story. One Christmas Eve, Martin Luther, while walking through a forest was moved by the beauty of the starlit fir trees. He was so moved that he brought one of the trees indoors and decorated it with candles to remind his children of God's creation.

Another story tells takes place in Germany. A Bremen guild chronicle from 1570 reports on how a small fir was decorated with apples, nuts, dates, pretzels and paper flowers. It was erected in the guild house, for the benefit of the guild members' children, who were allowed to collect the delectable food items on the morning of Christmas day.

Another early reference is from Basel, where a tailor apprentice carried around town a tree decorated with apples and cheese in 1597. He carried the tree to celebrate Jesus Christ's birth and to feed the needy people on Christmas morning.

By the mid 16th century, Christmas markets were set up every year in most German towns. These markets provided everything from gifts, food, and other practical gifts. At these markets, bakers made shaped gingerbreads and wax ornaments for people to buy as souvenirs. These souvenirs could be taken home and hung on the Christmas trees.

Many times the trees were symbolic of the tree in the Garden of Eden. Many food items were symbolic in nature. The ornamental flowers were originally only the colors red and white. The red color signified knowledge, while the color white stood for innocence and purity. The color white today still stands for innocence and purity, as it is the traditional color of a bride's wedding dress.

In the United States thanks to immigration of people from Germany, many Americans had adopted the Christmas tree custom by the late 18th Century. Several cities in the United States lay claim to erecting the country's first Christmas tree. Windsor

Locks, Connecticut, lays claim that a Hessian soldier put up a Christmas tree in 1777. He at that time was a prison of war imprisoned at the Noden-Reed House. The citizens of Windsor Locks lay claim to being the home of the first Christmas tree in New England. Also, the first Christmas tree in America is claimed by the town of Easton, Pennsylvania. German settlers erected a Christmas tree there back in 1816. To add even more debate to this issue, Matthew Zahm of Lancaster, Pennsylvania, recorded the use of a Christmas tree in 1821. This leads Lancaster to also lay claim to erecting the first Christmas tree in America.

Queen Victoria, as a child, was familiar with the custom of the Christmas tree. In her journal for Christmas Eve 1832, the delighted 13-year-old princess wrote, "After dinner...we then went into the drawing-room near the dining room. There were two large round tables on which were placed two trees, hung with lights and sugar ornaments. All the presents being placed round the trees...". After her marriage to her German cousin, Prince Albert, the custom became even more widespread.

In 1841, supposedly Prince Albert of Germany gave his wife, Queen Victoria of England, a gift of a Christmas tree. This was reputedly the first Christmas tree in England, but the custom spread quickly. The Monarchy in England set the precedent for style in Europe. It was kind of like keeping up with the Jones`. If the Monarchy had a tree, then everyone wanted a tree.

The generous Prince Albert also made gifts of Christmas trees to many schools throughout Great Britain. The Prince also had the army barracks decorated with trees at the time of Christmas. The soldiers could not be home with their families, but at least they could remember their families and have some holiday cheer. Images of the royal family with their Christmas tree at the Osborne House have been portrayed in many illustrations. The published images of the British Royal family at Christmas celebrations helped popularize the Christmas tree in Britain.

Chapter Three - Evolution of the Tree

In the mid-19th Century thanks to the popularity of the British Royalty, namely Queen Victoria and her German Prince Albert, the Christmas tree had an increase in popularity on a worldwide basis. As previously mentioned, many published pictures showed the royal couple standing with their children around a Christmas tree. Unlike most of the previous Royal family, Queen Victoria was very popular with her subjects. What the Queen did at Court became fashionable both in European and American Society. The English Christmas tree had arrived. Christmas tree decorations during that time period were still homemade. Some examples of these decorations are, quilled snowflakes, handmade stars, and paper baskets filled with sugared almonds and other edible goodies or candies. Small beaded decorations and silver tinsel originally came from Germany. Angels were designed for use at the top of the Christmas tree. By the 1860s, the English Christmas tree had become more innovative than the delicate trees of earlier times.

People hung small toys on the branches. Most gifts were placed on the table under the tree. The Christmas tree was spreading into other parts of Europe. The Mediterranean countries were not too interested in the tree.

In the late 19th Century, Christmas trees became a glorious hotchpotch of everything that could be decorated. This was in complete contrast to earlier times when the trees were decorated with delicate colors, shapes, and style. The size of the tree increased to floor standing trees, instead of the traditional smaller tree. In the earlier decades, the trees were usually table-sized trees.

Usually each person in the household had their own tree to decorate. The person would have all their own gifts placed on or under their tree. Thanks to decorations, along with crafts becoming more popular, the tree became a status symbol. The larger the tree the more affluent the family.

The Christmas tree of the 1890's was a child's joy to see. It would often be large enough to fill a room. The tree was most likely overwhelmed with glitter, tinsel, and toys. In England by the year 1900, themed trees had become very popular. A few examples of themed trees are those designed with a color theme set in ribbons, tinsel, or balls. A tree could have been designed as an Oriental Tree, or with an Egyptian theme was often desired. Unfortunately, Queen Victoria died in 1901 and England went into mourning. With her death, the fine trees of the time also departed.

In the 1930s, there was a revival of Dickensian nostalgia, especially in England. Christmas trees once again became large and were decorated with many bells, colorful balls, and shiny tinsels. The trees were often topped with a beautiful golden haired angel. Unfortunately, thanks to World War Two the large Christmas tree was once again gone. It became forbidden in England to cut trees down for decoration. Many people preferred to keep their precious Christmas tree decorations carefully stored away in metal boxes due to air raids. England went back to decorated small tabletop trees with homemade decorations. These trees were small enough that they could quickly be taken down into the air raid shelters for a little Christmas cheer.

After the war, England had a revival of the Christmas tree. The people needed the security of Christmas. In an ever-changing world, the Christmas tree was one of the few concrete symbols to help them get back on their feet.

The Christmas tree in America was slow to take off as a popular Christmas symbol. America is a large country unlike England, which is an small island in comparison. The people in the United States tended to have local customs, which were directly in relation to the immigrants who had settled in a particular area. It was not until mass media communications became widely available that the customs spread. The widespread use of newspapers and telegraphs in the 19th century helped to spread local customs across this vast continent. Thanks to poor mass media communication in the early part of this countries birth, references were hardly made regarding decorated Christmas trees in America, before the middle of the 19th century.

In the United States, it became a status symbol to have glass ornaments on the Christmas tree. The more glass ornaments a person displayed, the higher their esteemed social status. The United States was expanding. The popular tree topper was the Nation's Flag. At that time Christmas trees had became Patriotic. Christmas trees were imported into America sometime around 1880. Many were sold commercially through stores, such as FW Woolworth and Company.

The discovery of electricity was made by Benjamin Franklin in 1752, and although the study of electricity was just a hobby for Ben Franklin, he made many important scientific contributions. Later scientists, like Thomas A. Edison, continued to study electricity using many of Ben's ideas. There were a few American patents issued with regard to electricity. One such patent was for electric lights in 1882. Thomas Edison's assistant, Edward Johnson, developed the idea of Christmas tree lights that ran on electricity. This idea made indoor Christmas tree lights possible.

In turn, the possibility of indoor lights fostered the idea of using Christmas trees in outdoor displays. Another significant patent issued in 1892 was for metal hooks, which allowed for the safer hanging of decorations onto the trees.

Traditionally, Christmas trees in the past were not brought in and decorated until Christmas Eve. The trees were usually taken down the day after the twelfth night of Christmas, which is the 6th of January. Many people believed that to have a tree up before or after these dates brought bad luck. Modern commercialization of Christmas has resulted in trees being put up much earlier. In many stores trees are erected as early as late October. A common tradition in the United States is to put the tree up right after Thanksgiving. The tree will then be taken down right after the New Year. Some households in the U.S. do not put up the tree until the second week of December, and leave it up until the 6th of

January, which is the day of Epiphany. In Australia, the tradition of setting up the Christmas tree is for the Christmas tree to be erected on the 1st of December. This occurs about a week before the Australian students enjoy their school summer holidays.

So now, we have a basic idea of how the tree came to be used as a symbol. We also have learned why we use candles or lights on the trees. We also know that ornaments were originally delectable food items to be used as gifts on Christmas morning. In 1890, F.W. Woolworth brought the glass ornament tradition to the United States from Germany. German Artisans were known for their glass ornaments. At the time, F.W. Woolworth introduced the glass ornaments, there were over 5,000 different molds in use in Germany.

Another question that is still outstanding is, “What about tinsel?” All my research has shown that tinsel was used to enhance the lighting of the tree. It was to simulate shiny ice would could have been seen on an outdoor tree in the Winter season. Tinsel was invented in Germany around 1610. At that time, real silver was used in the production of tinsel. Machines were invented, which pulled the silver out into thin wafer strips. These thin strips were to be hung on the trees. Silver has always been symbolized as a pure substance. Many people believe silver can be used to ward off or fight evil. Many of man’s stories depict the use of silver to combat evil. Silver is very durable, but unfortunately, it tarnishes very quickly. To prevent tarnished tinsel many attempts were made to use a mixture of lead and tin. The biggest drawback to this creation was its weight. It was not practical as it was very heavy and the tree branches could not support the weight. Silver was used for tinsel right up to the mid-20th century.

Why do we light up the tree? Is the cause religious based? Well let me tell you all a little about the lights. The tradition of using small candles to light up a Christmas tree dates back to the middle of the 17th century. However, it took two centuries for the tradition to become widely established. It was first widely established in Germany and soon spread throughout Eastern Europe. Just like with the Christmas tree, immigrants brought the tradition to the United States. Originally, candles for the Christmas tree were glued with melted wax to a tree branch, or attached to a branch with pins. Around 1890, candle holders were first designed for use with the Christmas candles, but in 1902 small lanterns and glass balls to hold the candles were used.

As previously mentioned on December 22, 1882, Edward Johnson lit the first known electrically illuminated Christmas tree. He had the Christmas tree light bulbs especially made for him. He proudly displayed his Christmas tree, which was hand wired with 80 red, white, and blue electric incandescent light bulbs at his home on Fifth Avenue in New York City. He chose the colors from the American flag. He was being very Patriotic. Each of the bulbs was roughly the size of a walnut.

Thanks to his foresight, Edward Johnson has become widely recognized as the father of Electric Christmas Tree Lights.

The electric lights did not catch on in America until in 1895, when United States President Grover

Cleveland proudly sponsored the first electrically lit Christmas tree in the White House. It featured more than a hundred multicolored lights. The first commercially produced Christmas tree lights were manufactured in strings of multiples of eight light sockets by the General Electric Company of Harrison, New Jersey. It took until the mid 1950s for the use of multicolored electric lights to be adopted for use by the average household in the United States.

Today many strings of Christmas lights have found their way into other uses during the Christmas Season. They are used in places other than Christmas trees. Strings of lights adorn mantles and doorways inside homes, and are strung along the rafters, roof lines, and porch railings of homes and businesses.

Santa Claus has become increasingly familiar to most Americans. The Christmas tree has acquired tremendous popularity throughout all of North America. Many cities, towns, and department stores across the United States erect public Christmas trees indoors and outdoors for everyone to enjoy. If you do not have a tree you may very well be labeled a "Scrooge". The Rich's Great Tree in Atlanta, the Rockefeller Center Christmas Tree in New York City and the large Christmas tree at Victoria Square in Adelaide are all excellent examples of Community and National displays of Holiday cheer. In the United States, the National Christmas Tree is lit each year south of the White House in Washington, D.C.

Today, the lighting of the National Tree is part of what has become a major holiday event at the

White House. In 1979, President Jimmy Carter lit only the crowning star atop the Tree in honor of the Americans being held hostage in Iran. The very next year in 1980, the whole tree was fully lit for only 417 seconds. The rationale was that the tree was lit each second for each day the hostages had been in captivity.

A few hotels and other buildings will often string lights up from the roof to the top of a small tower on top of the building. This is done so that at night it appears as a lit Christmas tree. Also, they will often use green or other colored lights. Some skyscrapers will even go so far as to tell certain offices to leave their lights on and others off at night during December. This effect of the light placement will often appear from the ground as a Christmas tree pattern or some other holiday image.

In some cities tree lighting festivals are organized around the decoration and display of Christmas trees. These are usually conducted as charity events or Memorial events. In some cases the trees represent special commemorative gifts, such as in Trafalgar Square in London. The City of Oslo, Norway presents a tree each year to the people of London as a token of appreciation. This is done to thank the British for the their support of Norwegian resistance during the Second World War.

Chapter Four - Common Types of Trees

In today's modern society, both natural and artificial trees are used as Christmas trees. In this chapter I will discuss the common natural trees. In the next chapter, I will review the types and history of artificial trees.

Historians credit Mark Carr, a Catskill farmer in 1851 for creating the Christmas tree market. In 1851 he hauled two sleds of evergreen trees into New York City. Within fifty years twenty percent of American families had a Christmas tree and by the roaring 1920's most people had a Christmas tree.

In Europe, the most common species for use are the Firs. The major benefit of the Fir species is that they do not shed the needles as they dry out. The fir also provides good foliage color and scent. There are many other species that are also used. The most commonly used species in Europe are, the Silver Fir (the original species), Nordmann Fir, Noble Fir, Norway Spruce (generally the cheapest), Serbian Spruce, and the Scots Pine. Below you will find a brief description of each type of tree. The descriptions listed below come from Wikipedia Encyclopedia and the National Arbor Society. I received the information from their web site.

The Silver Fir is a large evergreen coniferous tree growing up to 40-50 m tall and with a trunk diameter of up to 1.5 m. The leaves are needle like, flattened, 1.8-3 cm long and 2 mm wide by 0.5 mm thick. They are glossy dark green in color. The tip of the leaf is usually slightly notched. The cones are 9-17 cm long and 3-4 cm broad, with about 150-200 scales per cone. The Silver Fir was the species first used as a Christmas tree. It has been largely replaced by the Nordmann Fir, which has denser, more attractive foliage.

The Nordmann Fir is a large evergreen coniferous tree that can grow up to 60 m tall. It has a trunk diameter of up to 2 m thick. The leaves are needle-like, flattened, 1.8-3.5 cm long and 2 mm wide by 0.5 mm thick, glossy dark green. The tip of the leaf is usually blunt, often slightly notched at the tip, but can be pointed, particularly on strong growing shoots on young trees. The cones are 10-20 cm long and 4-5 cm broad, with about 150-200 scales per cone. The Nordmann Fir is now one of the most important species grown for Christmas trees. It is favored for its attractive foliage. The needles are not sharp, nor do not drop readily when the tree dries out. It is also a popular ornamental tree used in parks and large gardens.

The Noble Fir is a large evergreen tree that typically grows up to 40-70 m tall and 2 m trunk diameter. The bark on the young trees is smooth, gray, and with resin blisters. As the tree matures the bark, becomes red brown, rough and fissured. The leaves are needle like, 1-3.5 cm long, blue green. They are arranged spirally on the shoot, but twisted slightly S shaped to be up curved above the shoot. The cones are erect, 11-22 cm long, with the purple scales almost completely hidden by the long yellow-green bract scales.

The Norway Spruce is a large evergreen coniferous tree that can grow to 35-55 m tall and with a trunk diameter of up to 1-1.5 m. Norway Spruce shoots are orange brown and hairless. The leaves are needle like, 12-24 mm long, quadrangular in cross section not flattened, and dark green on all four sides. The cones are 9-17 cm long, which are the longest of any spruce. They are green or reddish in color and turn brown when maturing 5-7 months after pollination. Norway Spruce is one of the most widely planted spruces. It is used in forestry for timber and paper production, and as an ornamental tree in parks and gardens. It is also widely planted for use as a Christmas tree. It is the cheapest Christmas tree to grow.

The Serbian Spruce is a medium-sized evergreen tree growing to 20-35 m tall with a trunk diameter of up to 1 m. The shoots are buff brown, and densely pubescent (hairy). The leaves are needle like, 10-20 mm long, flattened in cross section, and dark blue green in color. The cones are 4-7 cm long, fusiform (spindle shaped, broadest in the middle), dark purple (almost black) when young, maturing dark brown 5-7 months after pollination, and have stiff scales. Outside of its native range, Serbian Spruce is of major importance in horticulture as an ornamental tree in large gardens, valued in northern Europe and North America for its very attractive crown form and ability to grow on a wide range of soils. It is also grown to a small extent in forestry for Christmas trees.

The Scots Pine grows up to 25 m in height when mature. There are some 220-year-old trees that are 46 meters tall. The bark is thick, scaly dark gray brown on the lower trunk. While the bark is thin flaky and orange on the upper trunk and branches. The habit of the mature tree is distinctive due to its long, bare and straight trunk topped by a rounded or flat topped mass of foliage. On mature trees the leaves are an blue green, 3-5 cm long and occur in fascicles of two, but on young vigorous trees the leaves can be twice as long, and occasionally occur in threes and fours on the tips of strong shoots. The cones are pointed ovoid in shape and are 3-7 cm in length.

The Christmas trees generally used in North America are Balsam Fir, Fraser Fir, Grand Fir, Noble Fir, Red Fir, Douglas Fir, Scots Pine, and the Stone Pine. I will only describe the trees mentioned above. The first tree I will discuss is the Balsam Fir. The Balsam Fir is a medium sized tree generally reaching 40-60 feet in height and 1-1 1/2 feet in diameter. It exhibits a relatively dense, dark green pyramidal crown with a slender spire like tip. On its lower branches, the needles generally occur as two ranked (two rows along sides of the branch), being 3/4 - 1 1/2 inches long and spreading. On older branches, the needles tend to be shorter and curved upward, so as to cover the upper sides of the twigs. Individual needles are somewhat flat and may be blunt or notched at the end. Needles have a broad circular base and are usually dark green on the upper surface. As a Christmas tree, the balsam fir has several desirable properties. It has a dark green appearance, long lasting needles, and an attractive form. It also retains its pleasing fragrance.

The Fraser Fir is a coniferous tree, closely related to Balsam Fir. The Fraser Fir grows up to 25 m tall, 75 cm in trunk diameter and a 6-12 m spread. The crown is pyramidal with horizontal branches. It is dense when the tree is young, but becomes more open as it ages. The bark is gray brown and may become scaly with age. The bark is normally thin and smooth but usually has many resin blisters. The leaves are needle like, arranged spirally on the twigs but twisted at the base to spread in two rows. They are 12-25 mm long, flat and flexible with a rounded, notched tip, and dark green. The Fraser Fir is widely used as a Christmas tree. Its fragrance, appearance, and strong twigs. Its ability to retain its soft needles for a long time when cut make it an excellent choice for this purpose. The needles which do not prick easily when hanging ornaments make it also popular. In the past, it was also sometimes known as "She-balsam".

The Grand Fir is a large evergreen coniferous tree growing to 40-70 m tall and with a trunk diameter of up to 2 m. The leaves are needle-like, flattened, 3-6 cm long and 2 mm wide by 0.5 mm thick. They are glossy dark green and slightly notched at the tip. The leaf arrangement is spiral on the shoot, but with each leaf variably twisted at the base so they all lie in two more or less flat ranks on either side of the shoot. The cones are 6-12 cm long and 3.5-4.5 cm broad, with about 100-150 scales; the scale bracts are short, and hidden in the closed cone. The foliage has an attractive scent, and is sometimes used for Christmas decoration, including Christmas trees.

The Red Fir is a large evergreen tree typically up to 40-60 m tall and 2 m trunk diameter with a narrow conic crown. The bark on young trees is smooth, gray, and with resin blisters, becoming orange red, rough and fissured on old trees. The leaves are needle like, 2-3.5 cm long, glaucous blue green. They are arranged spirally on the shoot, but twisted slightly s-shaped to be up curved above the shoot. The cones are erect, 9-21 cm long, yellow-green, ripening brown. It is also a popular Christmas tree.

The Douglas Firs are medium-size to large or very large evergreen trees, to 20-100 m tall. The leaves are flat and needle like, generally resembling those of the firs. The female cones are pendulous, with persistent scales, and are distinct in having a long tridentine (three-pointed) bract that protrudes prominently above each scale. Douglas Fir wood is used for structural applications that require to withstand high loads.

The Stone Pine is a species of pine that has been exploited for its edible pine nuts, since prehistoric times. It is also a widespread horticultural tree, besides being cultivated for the seeds. The Stone Pine can exceed 25 m height, though is usually rather less tall, 12-20 m being more normal. It has a very characteristic shape, with a short trunk and very broad. The bark is thick, red brown and deeply fissured into broad vertical plates. The flexible mid green leaves are needle like, in bundles of two, and are 10-20 cm long. Young trees up to 5-10 years old bear juvenile leaves, which are very different, single (not paired), 2-4 cm long, and glaucous blue green in color. This tree has been used mostly in the United States as a table top Christmas tree.

Well, I find it pretty amazing when you look at all the types of trees that can be utilized for use as a Christmas tree. You probably, like me, originally thought a Christmas tree was simply a pine tree. As a child my family always stopped at a tree stand and bought a tree. I am pretty sure my parents did not consider the type of tree when purchasing a Christmas tree. My parents probably looked at the height, width, and overall shape of the tree, and bought the one they liked. There are a lot of people who buy a tree each year with the root ball so they can plant the tree after the holidays. This way they are not killing a tree. In a way each tree will hold special memories as they grow in their yard. In Chapter 6 you will learn all about planting and taking care of a tree with a root ball. The European tradition prefers the open aspect of naturally grown, unsheared tree, unlike in North America where there is a preference for close sheared trees with denser foliage. Unfortunately, the close sheared tree leaves less space to hang decorations. The shearing also damages the highly attractive natural symmetry of unsheared trees. In the past, Christmas trees were often harvested from wild forests, but now almost all are commercially grown on tree farms, especially in North America.

Almost all Christmas trees sold at Christmas in the United States are grown on Christmas tree farms. The trees are cut after about ten years of growth. New sapling trees are planted in their place. According to the United States Department of Agriculture (USDA) census for 2002, there were 21,904 farms producing conifers for the Christmas Tree market in America. In the United States, there are roughly 446,996 acres planted with Christmas Trees growing on them. There are 13,849 farms that harvest cut trees each year. The top 5 percent of the farms who are 100 acres or larger sold 61 percent of these trees. The top 26 percent of the farms which range from 20 acres to 100 acres sold 84 percent of the cut trees. Twenty one percent of the tree farms were less than two acres and sold an average of 115 trees per farm. Sounds like quite a big business.

Here is some interesting information that I have come across during my research. Christmas trees absorb carbon dioxide and emit fresh oxygen. This helps prevent the greenhouse effect that is so popularly discussed in the news. Each acre of Christmas trees produce the daily oxygen need for 18 people. There are approximately one million acres in use for growing Christmas trees in the United States. Theses trees produce enough oxygen for 18 million people on a daily basis. Unlike fake Christmas trees, which are often made in factories in other pats of the world, real Christmas trees are an all American business. Real Christmas trees are grown in all 50 states, including Hawaii and Alaska.

Chapter Five - Real vs. Fake Christmas Trees

Christmas trees come in a variety of sizes and shapes, such as the gigantic trees used at the White House and Rockefeller Center. There are even little artificial trees with an assortment of colored needles. Many families would not enjoy the Christmas season without a tree gracing their home.

Artificial trees have become increasingly popular. Some people consider them more convenient and they are able to be used for several years, they are less expensive than real trees. Artificial trees come in a number of colors and species. Some even come pre-decorated with lights. The convenience of the artificial tree is that at the end of the Christmas season the artificial tree can be disassembled and stored compactly for use next Christmas. To understand artificial Christmas trees we need first to look at their history and the types that man has created over time.

The first artificial trees were tabletop feather trees. These were made from green dyed goose feathers that were attached to a wooden pole to simulate a tree trunk. The feathers were wound onto sticks drilled into a larger one, like the branches on a tree. These trees originated in Germany in the 19th century. The use of the goose feather tree came about as the people in Germany tried to prevent further deforestation. The first feather trees came to the U.S. in 1913. They were sold in the Sears, Roebuck, and Company catalog.

In America, the Addis Brush Company created the first brush style trees. The Brush Company used the same machinery that made their toilet brushes. These trees had an tremendous advantage over feather trees. They could handle heavier decorations and were not as flammable. Addis Brush Trees became popular in Britain and were being imported in significant quantity. The trees became immensely popular for a time. However, the favorites were still real trees. In South Wales, where real trees were often difficult to find especially in the rural areas, Holly Bushes were often decorated for use as a Christmas tree.

The first artificial trees sold that were not green in color were the metallic trees. These were first introduced about 1958. They became quite popular through the 1960s. These trees were made of aluminum which was attached to metal rods, and supported on wooden or aluminum central poles. Some of the trees were made with aluminum coated paper, which unfortunately was extremely flammable. They were a fire hazard if the tree lights came to rest directly on the paper. Warnings to this effect are still issued with some Christmas tree lights today to help prevent house fires. More recent tinsel trees can be used safely with lights due to the use of flame retardant materials as well as improvements in the safety of the Christmas tree lights themselves. In Chapter Six I will discuss in detail home safety with regard to Christmas trees and lighting.

The United States in the 1970's returned to the nostalgia of the Victorian age. It was a decade later that Britain followed this fashion style. At first the Victorian style was a refreshing look, and manufacturers, realizing the sales potential, began to create more and more fantastic decorations. Some American companies even began to specialize in antique replicas. They recreated many wonderful glass ornaments, real silver tinsels and pressed foil Dresdens. A Dresden is a die cut embossed paper ornament originally made in Germany in the 19th century.

In the 1980s in the United States, some trees were sprayed with fluffy white flocking to simulate snow. Typically it would be sprayed all over the tree from all sides, which would produce a look different from real snow. Flocking is done with a professional sprayer at a tree lot or by the manufacturer if it is an artificial tree. It can be done at home from a spray can, but it can be messy.

Since the late 1990s, many indoor artificial trees have come pre-strung with lights. Some also come lit partially or completely by fiber optics. The lights are often located in the base. The base also contains a rotating color wheel which causes the various colors to shimmer across the tree. Past gimmicks to get consumers to purchase an artificial tree included talking or singing trees. Trees have even been designed to blow "fake snow" over themselves. The “fake snow” is actually small Styrofoam beads. The beads collect in a decorative cardboard bin at the bottom of the tree where they are blown back up to the top through a tube hidden next to the trunk. Some supermarket chains even offer conifer seedlings sold with cheap decorations attached by soft pipe cleaners. Real potted ones are often sold like this, and artificial ones often come with decorations.

In 2005, inverted Christmas trees became very popular. They were originally sold as decoration displays for merchants. This design was planned to allow customers to get closer to the ornaments that were being sold. However, the customers enjoyed the design. They then desired to buy the inverted tree for their own home use. Many retailers also claimed that the trees were popular, because they allowed larger presents to be placed beneath the trees. Honestly, who doesn't want bigger and/or more presents under their tree?

There is some debate as to whether artificial or real trees are better for the natural environment. Many artificial trees are made out of PVC, which can be a toxic material. PVC is often stabilized with lead, which is a known carcinogen and can cause birth defects. Some trees have a warning that the dust or leaves from the tree should not be eaten or inhaled. Sounds like a tree I wouldn't want in my home. A small amount of real tree material is used in some artificial trees. For example, the bark of a real tree can be used to surface an artificial trunk or its branches. Polyethylene trees are less toxic, but more expensive, than PVC trees. Artificial trees can be used for many years, but are not recyclable. They eventually end up in landfills.

Real trees without a root ball are used only for a short time, but can be recycled and used as mulch or used to prevent erosion. In Massachusetts, there are naturalists who often use the natural trees as a break to save the sand dunes along the ocean shoreline. Real trees also help reduce the amount of carbon dioxide in the atmosphere while growing. Live trees are typically grown as a crop and replanted in rotation after cutting. This also often provides a suitable habitat for wildlife. Many people also decorate their outdoor trees with food that birds along with other wildlife can eat and enjoy. Some examples are; garlands made from unsalted popcorn or cranberries, pine cones covered with peanut butter rolled in bird seed, orange halves, and seed covered suet cakes. Many people enjoy feeding and watching the birds during the Winter season.

Real Christmas trees are popular, but many homeowners prefer the convenience of the authentic looking artificial tree, which is manufactured. Depending on the size of the room you are using for your tree, you could have a 14-foot artificial Spruce right there in your living room. The best part is that you will not have a single dropped needle. The new trees are so realistic that you can fool anyone at first glance. Thanks to modern chemistry, there are even pine-scented sprays to use on the tree for that real tree smell.

To sum it all up, always consider some important facts when buying your Christmas tree. Fake trees and wreaths are made from nonrenewable petroleum products, unlike real trees which are renewable and biodegradable. Secondly if a fake tree catches fire it releases dangerous toxic fumes, where as a real tree's smoke is not toxic. Fake trees cannot be recycled when they are thrown out. They are not biodegradable and will not disintegrate. Lastly as previously mentioned, fake trees are made mostly outside of the United States, which means our economy is affected through the loss of jobs by American labor.

Whether you decide to buy a live tree or an artificial tree, it will inspire many good thoughts and memories. Looking back to when I was a child with regard to setting up the tree, my father and I brought the tree into the living room and set it up. We centered it and strung the multi-colored lights and my mother's duty was to hang each ornament with care. To this day she has many memories regarding the tree. She will pick up an ornament and tell my children a story of who and when it was given to her. Some of the people have passed away, but their memory resides in a tiny Christmas ornament.

Chapter Six - The Wreath and Other Goodies

No book about Christmas trees would be complete if it did not talk about wreathes. Today's wreathes are mostly constructed of evergreen branches, pretty colored bows, pine cones, holly, and any other item that a person could desire. It is pretty amazing how a few evergreen pine boughs can be transformed into an object of beauty. Read on and learn all about the wreath.

The making of wreaths is an ancient and honored art that began about a thousand years before the birth of Christ. The Christmas Wreath symbolizes the strength of life while overcoming the forces of winter. The wreath is a Pagan symbol of immortality. The circle and sphere are symbols of immortality. The use of evergreens and wreaths as symbols of life was an ancient custom of the Egyptians, Chinese, and Hebrews.

The wreath has a long history. Many religions used the wreath in religious celebrations. Originally, the circlet was known as a "diadem". The circlet was often formed out of fabric in headbands, which were sometimes adorned with jewels. In 776 B.C., wreaths made of laurel leaves were used to crown the victors of the Olympic Games. As the Olympic Games rotated to different cities, the wreaths took on different styles. Each host city would construct the award head garlands from branches of their local trees. The god Apollo is often depicted wearing or holding a wreath of laurel leaves.

In Ancient Roman times wreaths were festive crowns. Wreaths were usually for women, while the men usually wore crowns. The wreath was used as a symbol of pride, and they were often handmade. Most of the wreaths were made from local flowers, tree branches, twigs, colored threads, and laurels. Wreaths also were often used on special occasions, such as a weddings. Laurel wreaths were worn on the heads of military and government officials in parades. Roman consuls and senators wore wreaths of olive leaves in public as a sign of the prestige of their position in society. Funeral wreaths were also a Roman custom.

It is unknown when in history people transitioned wreaths from head ornament to use as a wall decoration. Beautifully decorated wreaths are an integral part of the December holidays, but they have become popular throughout the year. People often decorate a wreath to fit each season.

The use of evergreens for Christmas wreaths and other decorations most likely originated in northern Europe, Italy and Spain sometime in the early 19th century. The traditional colors of Christmas are green and red. Green is used to represent the continuance of life through the winter. It also reinforces the Christian belief of an eternal life through Jesus Christ. Red symbolizes the blood that Jesus shed at his crucifixion to save mankind from sin. For most people the word "wreath" simply conjures visions of rings of evergreens with red ribbons hung on doors at Christmas.

The origins of the Advent wreath are hypothesized to be from the folk practices of the Pagan Germanic people. During the cold December darkness of Eastern Europe, they gathered wreaths of evergreen, and lighted fires as signs of hope in a coming spring and renewed light.

Perhaps the loveliest use of this symbol is the Advent wreath. This wreath is made mostly from evergreen tree twigs, that are sometimes decorated with pinecones and a bow made of red ribbon. This is a common Christmas decoration. Christians have kept these popular traditions alive.

By the 16th century, Catholics and Protestants throughout Germany used these symbols to celebrate their Advent hope in Christ, the everlasting Light. From Germany, the use of the Advent wreath spread to other parts of the Christian world. The wreath is made of four candles in a circle of evergreens with a fifth candle in the middle. Three candles are violet in color and the fourth is the color pink. Sometimes four white candles or four violet candles can also be used. Each day at home, the candles are lit. One candle during the first week, and then another each succeeding week until December 25th. A short prayer may accompany the lighting of each candle. The last candle is the middle candle. The lighting of this candle takes place on Christmas Eve. It represents Jesus Christ being born. The traditional Christmas wreath is hung anytime from right after Thanksgiving to mid-December and left hanging through the winter months. Decorating a wreath is a matter of personal taste. Many have electric lights. There are even some commercially made with fiber optics that change colors.

Almost everyone has heard of Mistletoe. I do not think that there is a plant around that has sparked as much humor as Mistletoe. The vines and berries of mistletoe were sacred to the ancient Druids. They used them in their sacrifices to the gods. They were also used to help celebrate the winter solstice. Traditionally the Druid priest would be dressed in white robes. The priest would go into the forest in the dead of night and climb trees to cut clusters of mistletoe with silver and gold sickles.

The mistletoe was also believed to have miraculous healing powers. It was often placed over doorways to ward off evil and bestow health, happiness, and good luck to those dwelling inside the shelter. As hugs of welcome usually occur at a doorway, the custom evolved into balls of greens and berries hung wherever an enterprising boy might surprise his girl. In eighteenth century England, kissing balls were made of evergreens, ribbons, and ornaments with sprigs of mistletoe tied to the bottoms of the balls.

The ancient Druids also believed that the Holly bush was sacred, possibly because it was an evergreen and therefore favored by the sun. Being sacred meant being inhabited by spirits, so the Druids would bring some holly branches indoors in winter to give the spirits shelter from the hardships outside and gain their favor and good luck.

Holly was also believed to have magical powers to drive demons away. To this day, there are some people who consider holly to be a good luck charm against the hostile forces of nature, much like rubbing a rabbit's foot, which is said to bring good luck. When sprigs of holly were tied to bedposts, it was believed to guard against ghosts and demons. There are some people who plant Holly around their windows to keep prying eyes and possible intruders away. The leaves are very prickly and can be painful against skin.

The legend of Santa Claus began in the fourth century with a man known as Nicholas, who at that time was the Bishop of Myra. He lived in a part of Asia Minor. Currently that part of Asia Minor is known as the country, Turkey. He was renowned for his wisdom, charity, generosity, and compassion. He supposedly gave all his money to helping the poor. He was very rich, generous, and loving toward children. Often, he gave joy to poor children by throwing gifts in through their windows as he rode by or by sneaking in to their homes while they slept.

One early legend relates how Nicholas helped save the three daughters of a poor man. Nicholas reportedly tossed bags of gold through a window of the family's home on three separate occasions. He did this to give each woman a worthy dowry, which would attract a suitable husband. This would enable each daughter to gain an honorable marriage and help them avoid being sold off as slaves. The ideal of the saint as a mysterious bearer of gifts in the middle of the night may have its origins in this story. Various cultures around the world have evolved over time their own stories of a gift-bearing being.

The American version of the Santa Claus figure received its inspiration and its name from the Dutch legend of Sinter Klaas. This legend was first brought to the United States of America by Dutch immigrants. Sinter Klaas was known to travel with an elf, called Black Peter. This elf would punish disobedient children. This occurred in New York during the late 17th century. In 1773, the Sinter Klaas name appeared in the American press as "St. A Claus". It was the popular author, Washington Irving who gave Americans their first detailed information about the Dutch version of Saint Nicholas. In his book the "History of New York", he described the arrival of the gift bearing Saint on horseback each Eve of Christmas.

"The Night Before Christmas" written by Clement Clarke Moore helped open a multitude of people's minds to this Dutch Saint Nick. In his work, Clement Clarke Moore included such details as the names of all the reindeer that pulled Saint Nick's sled. Santa was rumored to fly over housetops in a reindeer drawn sleigh. Clement Clarke Moore also described Santa Claus's laugh, winks, and nods. This was the first mentioning ever of Saint Nicholas as an elf. This story also described how Santa could go down and return up the chimney.

At first, the image of Saint Nicholas began as a thin rather stern looking bishop. Think about it for a moment. Honestly, who believed or wanted a stern person bringing them gifts? As times changed so did Santa's image, to that of a rotund, jolly pleasant fellow. In 1863, a caricaturist for Harper's Weekly, named Thomas Nast developed his own image of Santa Claus. Thomas Nast designed his Santa as a figure with a flowing set of whiskers. His portrayal of Santa showed him dressed all in fur. He also described a Santa that lived at the North Pole and was assisted by elves, who made toys to be delivered to good boys and girls on Christmas Eve. Thomas Nast's 1866 montage, entitled "Santa Claus and His Works" established Santa as a maker of toys. In 1869, a book of the same name collected Nast's drawings. This book included a poem written by George P. Webster that identified the North Pole as Santa's home.

The jolly old St. Nick that we know and love today has evolved over time from many countless images. These images did not come from folklore. In the 1920s, the artist Haddon Sundblom created a series of advertisements for Coca-Cola and Company. In the advertisements, Santa wears the Companies' corporate colors, which are now known worldwide as red and white. In the advertisements, he portrayed Santa Claus with a heavy, rotund belly, white beard, and mustache. Santa also had crinkled eyes and rosy checks. These ads finally fully changed the image of St. Nicholas to one as a plump and kindly old elf. This image is still the one we know today.

The New York Times reported a description of Santa Claus on 27 November 1927. Their description said, "A standardized Santa Claus appears to New York children. Height, weight, stature are almost exactly standardized, as are the red garments, the hood and the white whiskers. The pack full of toys, ruddy cheeks and nose, bushy eyebrows and a jolly, paunchy effect are also inevitable parts of the requisite make-up".

In the movie, A Miracle on 34th Street, the character known as Kris Kringle, also known as Santa Clause is further embedded as a gentle kind and giving person into our minds. He is caring, honest, cheerful, and cares about his fellow beings. The character looks very similar to the Santa from the Coca Cola and Company advertisements. He is Grand-fatherly in appearance with a white beard. He is rotund and has a great laugh. This further cements into our societies mind the true current image of Santa. Movies at that time and eventually television would mold how the world viewed Christmas and the Holiday Season. If it was displayed in the newspaper, shown on the big screen or the television set, it was probably true.

Christmas and Santa are so fun filled that people have capitalized on them. In Alaska, there is a recreational vehicle campground called, Santaland. It is a delightfully unique, Christmas-themed park located in the heart of North Pole, Alaska's Christmas City! The park boasts of displaying a fiberglass Santa Claus that is 42 feet tall, with a girth of 33 feet at the waste. Santa weighs 900 pounds. Santa was built in 1968 by Wes Stanley of Stanley Plastics in Enumclaw, Washington.

The State of Indiana has a town called Santa Claus. The town of Santa Claus, Indiana, was named on Christmas Eve in 1852. As of the 2000 census, the town population was 2,041, not including Elves. Milton Harris an entrepreneur, created Santa's Candy Castle which was the first tourist attraction in Santa Claus, Indiana. Santa's Candy Castle is also purported to be the first themed attraction in the United States. Santa Claus Town attractions also include a red-brick Candy Castle, sponsored by Curtiss Candy. This was dedicated on

December 22, 1935. The town has a Toy Village, which is a series of miniature fairytale buildings. They are sponsored by prominent national toy manufacturers. Santa Claus Town led to the creation of the town's first newspaper, "The Santa Claus Town News", and the Santa Claus Chamber of Commerce.

In the Adirondack Mountains near Lake Placid is a town called, North Pole. At the North Pole in New York, there is a theme park, called Santa's Workshop. The magic of Christmas comes alive again when you visit Santa Claus at his home and workshop. The village is nestled on the side of Whiteface Mountain. Founded in 1949 and designed by Arto Monaco. The post office at Santa's Workshop guarantees delivery of the bags stuffed full of letters from children across the globe to Santa. Any piece of mail that is sent in the eastern United States that is addressed to Santa Claus or the North Pole usually makes its way to Santa here at Santa's Workshop in North Pole, New York.

Santa's Workshop has a special program called, Santa's Operation Toylift. This operation delivers toys and gifts to underprivileged children. Originally, the toys were delivered in northern New York and Vermont with pilot Julian Reiss and his personal aircraft. With the help of a C-46 called, "the Silver Sleigh" which was provided by ESSO Standard Oil of New Jersey, Operation Toylift has expanded to over 13 States, The District of Columbia, and two Provinces of Canada. The Silver Sleigh makes 34 stops at major airports delivering over ten tons of presents to orphaned children.

It would be unforgivable if I did not discuss Christmas cards. As a child I would watch my mother filling out what seemed like an endless supply of cards to be sent to immediate family, relatives, friends, and my father's business associates. Not once did I ever wonder why. Thanks to today's modern technology, people now send electronic Christmas cards. However, I am a little old fashioned, I still enjoy the thrill of ripping open an envelope and physically holding the card as I read it.

Why do we fill out Christmas cards each year? Where did this idea start? Did this tradition originate from a country? Read on and I will help clear the air on this topic. The tradition of sending Christmas cards became an accepted custom during the 19th century. From the 5th through the 15th century, many Europeans would exchange wooden prints of religious themes during the Christmas holiday. John Horsley, an English illustrator in 1843, created the first modern Christmas card. This first card depicted a family Christmas celebration. It read, "A Merry Christmas and a Happy New Year to You". In 1875, Louis Prang, a printer in the United States made some advances in color lithography that made mass produced Christmas cards possible. Thanks to his card making process, the custom of exchanging Christmas cards soon spread throughout the country.

Chapter Seven - Real Tree Care

As a Registered Nurse, I would be irresponsible if I did not discuss real tree care and holiday safety. So, you have returned safely home with your Christmas tree. Now what do you expect? The continued fresh appearance depends upon the type of care you provide.

Are you thinking about planting some evergreen trees or your families Christmas tree? Do you simply want the Christmas tree for decoration and then have it thrown out. This chapter will help you take care of either tree. Evergreen trees are saviors in winter, who deserve of our tender care. Their foliage brightens the winter landscape and affords windbreaks that help save us money on our fuel bills.

The first thing to do after you have bought your Christmas tree is to get it home and into a water filled stand as quickly as possible. A Christmas tree should never be mounted dry, but rather be kept in a container filled with clean water that is replenished on a regular basis. Depending upon the size, species, and location of the tree, it may absorb up to a gallon of water within the first day. The tree's water should be checked frequently and maintained as necessary. Some people advocate placing various substances in the water to preserve freshness. I recommend that consumers simply keep the tree well watered with pure tap water. No messy chemicals or additives are necessary. As long as the tree is able to absorb and transpire water, it will be reasonably fire resistant.

When a Christmas tree is cut, over half of its weight is water. With proper care, you can maintain the quality of your displayed trees. Below are a number of tips relating to the care of displayed trees. Displaying trees in water in a traditional reservoir type stand is the most effective way of maintaining their freshness and minimizing needle loss problems. Once home, the tree should be placed in water as soon as possible. Most species can go 6 to 8 hours after cutting the trunk and still take up water. There are now even some devices available that help maintain a constant water level in its stand, so you never have to worry about watering your Christmas tree. Always avoid whittling the sides of the trunk down to fit a stand as this impedes the ability of the tree from taking up water. The water temperature used to fill the stand does not affect water uptake. Check the stand daily to make sure that the level of water does not go below the base of the tree. There can still be water in the stand even though the base of the tree is no longer submerged in water. Monitor the tree for freshness. After Christmas, or if at any time the tree is dry, remove it from the house.

Using a small handsaw, cut about an inch off the bottom of the tree trunk at a slight angle to aid water absorption. This removes any clogged wood that may not readily absorb the fresh water. Make sure the tree is mounted securely in its stand, and that the tree itself is positioned away from open flames or heat sources, which may dry it out prematurely.

I cannot repeat this enough, but once again it is important that the tree should always be kept watered and not allowed to dry out. If the tree does become dried out, it may not be able to adequately absorb moisture once it is re-watered. This will cause it to shed its needles prematurely. If this happens, take the tree down and cut about a 1 inch slice off the bottom of the trunk. Replacing the tree in the stand and re-water it. This should remedy the problem. Although inconvenient, especially if your tree is fully decorated, it is the only way to prevent early needle loss.

A good rule of thumb is to treat a green Christmas tree just like a fresh bouquet of cut flowers. You most likely have spent a nice bit of money on your tree. Most trees can cost upwards of one hundred dollars. The bigger the tree the higher the cost. Think of your tree as a Christmas investment. After your tree has been mounted, the decorating can begin.

You may have decided to buy a Christmas tree with a root ball. You plan on putting it in the ground and watching it and the Christmas memories grow. How do you do it? What care is needed? Do you have to do anything special? Read on and follow the tips mentioned below and you are sure to have a beautiful tree in your yard for many decades of decorating for Christmas. Here are some tips for planting live Christmas trees.

First, you should dig the hole in the ground for planting well before Christmas. This is important so you will not have to dig through frozen dirt. Digging is hard enough without going through frozen earth.

Bring the dirt that you remove from the hole inside, to keep it from freezing. Keeping it in a garage or other enclosed shelter is perfectly acceptable. Do not forget that, as a living plant, your tree will need to be watered on regular basis. Always keep the root ball damp. The tree while in the house should avoid being exposed to extreme temperature fluctuations. Try to place the tree in the coolest spot that you can find in the house. This will help prevent the tree from drying out.

The tree will need to go through a transitional period starting the day after Christmas. This period should last for about two weeks. The tree needs to get out of the warm house, but it should not be put out into freezing temperatures right away, otherwise you may shock it and kill it. A garage attached to a house or an enclosed unheated porch would be the ideal storage facility for the tree, during this transitional period.

When it is time to plant the tree, the very top of the root ball should be level with the ground. If the roots come wrapped in any material, for example burlap, then it should be removed. Water the newly planted tree and apply mulch. Do not pile the mulch up against the trunk. About 3" of mulch is more than enough. Too much is worse than not mulching at all. Your job is done. You, your friends, and family will now have a gift in your yard that will keep on giving.

Chapter Eight – Christmas Safety

There is nothing worse than having a fire break out and ruin your home at anytime of the year. Having it happen during the Holiday Season always feels much worse. Here are some indoor safety tips.

A properly maintained Christmas tree is not a particular fire hazard, but common sense is important. The Christmas tree should be located in a safe place, preferably near a wall or corner where it is not likely to be knocked over by children or pets. Keeping the tree away from heat sources such as hot air ducts, wood stoves, fireplaces, etc., will help to preserve its freshness and lessen any fire danger. Candles or open flame ornaments of any kind should never ever be used. Check strings of lights to ensure that the bulbs are working properly, and that the cords are not frayed. One of my favorite quotes is, "If in doubt, chuck them out". Make sure all the connections are secure. Discard any light strands that look questionable and replace with new strands. Never leave the tree lights on when no one is at home. Once your tree is up and decorated, sit back and enjoy.

The majority of Christmas lights manufactured today use a parallel wiring system. Parallel wiring systems provide more than one path of electricity for each light bulb to follow. After the current leaves the light bulb, it follows two or more paths before returning to the original electrical source. The parallel lights have two wires and each light bulb has its own positive and negative wire connection.

If one light bulb burns out, the rest of the lights will remain lit. To reduce the risk of overheating the lights, you should always replace any burned out light bulbs promptly. Always use the same wattage replacement bulb as the original bulb. The voltage of the lights does not change when another set of lights are added. Too much current flowing through the electrical wires and the light bulbs will cause excess heat, which will cause the light bulbs to burn out sooner. Fortunately, today's lights are equipped with a fuse that limits the amount of current that will pass through the lights. Over heating of electrical wires can cause electrical fires.

When using Christmas tree lights, basic precautions should always be followed. Use only UL approved Christmas tree lights. Check for frayed wires and broken sockets. Get rid of any damaged sets. Do not try to fix them. Overall their price is cheap. They can shock a person or start a fire. No more than three light sets should be used on any one extension cord. Extension cords should be placed against the wall to avoid tripping hazards, and do not run cords under rugs.

Never use outdoor lights on an indoor Christmas tree as they might create too much heat.

Lights should never touch any combustible materials. Do not overload electrical outlets. Never use more than three strings of lights on any one electrical circuit. Lights should not be used on artificial trees with metal frames as they can cause shocks if any wires are frayed. Miniature lights are safer because they produce less heat. They are also more energy efficient.

Never leave the lights on when going to bed or leaving the house. Keep candles with real flames away from Christmas trees.

Never use candles as tree decorations.

When decorating the tree, place breakable ornaments on the higher limbs. Using the higher limbs will protect your children and pets as well as safeguard the breakables. Use flame resistant decorations. Keep small ornaments that can be swallowed away from small children and pets. They could be a choking hazard. Place tinsel higher on the tree out of reach of children and pets. If swallowed, it is also a choking hazard. Use non-flammable holders for candles. Keep them out of reach of children and pets. Do not leave the lights lit when going to bed or leaving the house.

Here are some safety tips for Outdoor Christmas Tree Lights. First of all, have a certified electrician install a GFCI outlet, if you do not already have one. Make sure the product is intended to be used for outdoor Christmas tree lighting. Always follow all the manufacturer's instructions and precautions. Any extension cords used for outdoor Christmas tree lights should also be intended specifically for use outside.

Water and electricity do not mix, so keep any connections out of the snow or puddles and insert bulbs into sockets such that the sockets point down.

Always unplug any outdoor Christmas lights before replacing a burnt out bulb. Don't string outdoor Christmas tree lights on trees that come into contact with power lines. If you are reusing old outdoor Christmas tree lights, please inspect the wires to ensure that there are no wear spots.

It is not only fire hazards that you should watch out for during the holiday season. November is the peak month for falls from ladders. Whether it's cleaning out gutters or setting up Christmas decorations. Ladder falls send more people to hospital emergency departments in the month before Christmas than for any other cause. People between 40 and 59 accounted for nearly half the visits. Men made up more than half of emergency room patients who were injured by falling from a ladder. Always use the proper step stool or ladder to reach high places.

Conclusion

After all my research, I was amazed at how little is known about this very popular symbol of Christmas. After reading many stories and doing a tremendous amount of research, I honestly believe it did originate as a Pagan worship symbol. Saint Boniface in all my research is the first documented person to use the Fir tree to explain Christianity. The use of the Christmas tree has evolved over the centuries. It has gone from a simple tree with homemade baked goods to today's tree surrounded by presents.

The true meaning behind Christmas and the tree seems to be lost at times. When I was a child, it was taboo for any store to have Christmas decorations setup until after Thanksgiving. Every year, thanks to Corporate America, the decorations are setup earlier and earlier. In fact, this year I was in a National Chain that had Christmas trees setup right next to the Halloween candies. At what point do we draw the line?

I was in a mall around the Holidays and just for fun, I asked 25 assorted people of varying ages a simple question. The question was, "What is the first thing that comes to mind when I mention Christmas?". Twelve people answered Santa Claus. Seven people answered the Christmas tree. Four people replied the birth of their Savior, Jesus Christ, and two replied credit card debt. Granted this was a small group of people and in no way can it be seen as a true representation of how people look at the Christmas Season. I just thought it was interesting. One person asked not to be in the little survey as they are of the Jewish faith. However, the person did tell me that their father owned a toy store in Brooklyn, New York when they were a child. Every year on Christmas Day, their father would have the store open for any parent who needed a last minute gift. After all, Christmas was not their religious holiday. After closing the store on Christmas, the person's father could often be heard saying, "What a Friend I Have in Jesus", as he counted out his cash register.

Hollywood has even given society a term for a sad looking tree. The term "Charlie Brown Christmas tree" is often used to describe any sad looking, malformed little tree. Some tree buyers intentionally adopt such trees. They may feel sympathetic to the trees plight or want to say simply that they have a "Charlie Brown tree". This term comes from the appearance of Charlie Brown's Christmas tree in the TV special, A Charlie Brown Christmas.

Resources

Britannica Encyclopedia
331 North La Salle Street
Chicago, IL 60610
www.Britannica.com

National Safety Council
1121 Spring Lake Drive
Itasca, IL 60143-3201
(630) 285-1121
(630) 285-1315 fax
info@nsc.org

Santa's Workshop
PO Box 1768
North Pole, NY 12997
1-800-806-0215
info@northpoleny.com
www.northpoleny.com

Santaland RV Park
125 St. Nicholas Dr.
North Pole, Alaska 99705
1-888-488-9123
www.santalandrv.com

The National Arbor Day Foundation
100 Arbor Avenue
Nebraska City, NE 68410
Toll Free: 1-888-448-7337

www.arborday.org

University of Indiana
107 S. Indiana Ave.,
Bloomington, IN 47405-7000
(812) 855-4848
www.indiana.edu/earthrel/paganfaq.html

Virginia Cooperative Extension
110 Hutcheson Hall
Virginia Tech
Blacksburg, VA 24061
540-231-1247
www.ext.vt.edu

Wikipedia Encyclopedia
200 2nd Ave. South #358
St. Petersburg, FL 33701-4313
www.wikipedia.org

Glossary

Advent - the period beginning four Sundays before Christmas, observed in commemoration of the coming of Christ into the world.

All Saints Day - a church festival celebrated November 1 in honor of all the saints.

Apollo - the ancient Greek and Roman god of light, healing, music, poetry, prophecy, and manly beauty.

Asia Minor - a peninsula in W Asia between the Black and Mediterranean seas, including most of Asiatic Turkey.

Bible - the sacred writings of the Christian religion.

Bishop - a person who supervises a number of local churches or a diocese, being in the Greek, Roman Catholic, Anglican, and other churches a member of the highest order of the ministry.

Boniface - English monk who became a missionary in Germany.

Carter, Jimmy - 39th President of the United States.

Catholic - pertaining to the whole Christian body or church.

Chinese - a native or descendant of a native of China.

Christian - a person who believes in Jesus Christ; adherent of Christianity.

Christianization - to make Christian; to imbue with Christian principles.
Christmas - the annual festival of the Christian church commemorating the birth of Jesus: celebrated on December 25 and now generally observed as a legal holiday and an occasion for exchanging gifts.

Constantine - Roman emperor.

Date - the oblong, fleshy fruit of the date palm, a staple food in northern Africa, Arabia.

Diadem - a crown.

Druid - A member of an order of priests in ancient Gaul and Britain who appear in Welsh and Irish legend as prophets and sorcerers.

Easter - an annual Christian festival in commemoration of the resurrection of Jesus Christ, observed on the first Sunday after the first full moon after the vernal equinox, as calculated according to tables based in Western churches on the Gregorian calendar and in Orthodox churches on the Julian calendar.

Edison, Thomas - United States inventor; inventions included the phonograph and incandescent electric light and the microphone and the Kinetoscope.

Egyptian - a native or inhabitant of Egypt.

Electrician - a person who installs, operates, maintains, or repairs electric devices or electrical wiring.

Elf - one of a class of preternatural beings, esp. from mountainous regions, with magical powers, given to capricious and often mischievous interference in human affairs, and usually imagined to be a diminutive being in human form; sprite; fairy.

Evergreen - having green leaves throughout the entire year, the leaves of the past season not being shed until after the new foliage has been completely formed.

Extension Cord - an electric cord having a standard plug at one end and a standard electric jack at the other.

Franklin, Benjamin - American statesman, diplomat, author, scientist, and inventor.

Garden of Eden - The garden of God and the first home of Adam and Eve.

Germanic - a native or inhabitant of Germany.

GFCI Outlet - ground fault circuit interrupter.

Gospel - the story of Christ's life and teachings, esp. as contained in the first four books of the New Testament, namely Matthew, Mark, Luke, and John.

Hebrew - the story of Christ's life and teachings, esp. as contained in the first four books of the New Testament, namely Matthew, Mark, Luke, and John.

Hessian - a Hessian mercenary used by England during the American Revolution.

Holly - any of numerous trees or shrubs of the genus Ilex, as opaca (American holly), the state tree of Delaware, or I. aquifolium (English holly), having glossy, spiny-toothed leaves, small, whitish flowers, and red berries; foliage and berries used for decoration, esp. during the Christmas season.

Immigration - To enter and settle in a country or region to which one is not native.

Immortality - Endless life or existence.

Jesus Christ - Jesus of Nazareth. born 4? b.c., crucified a.d. 29? the source of Christian religion.

Ladder - a structure of wood, metal, or rope, commonly consisting of two sidepieces between which a series of bars or rungs are set at suitable distances, forming a means of climbing up or down.

Medieval - of, pertaining to, characteristic of, or in the style of the Middle Ages:

Mistletoe - a European plant, *Viscum album,* having yellowish flowers and white berries, growing parasitically on various trees, used in Christmas decorations.

Monarchy - supreme power or sovereignty held by a single person.

Monk - a man who has withdrawn from the world for religious reasons, esp. as a member of an order of cenobites living according to a particular rule and under vows of poverty, chastity, and obedience.

Mulch - a covering, as of straw, compost, or plastic sheeting, spread on the ground around plants to prevent excessive evaporation or erosion, enrich the soil, inhibit weed growth.

North Pole - the end of the earth's axis of rotation, marking the northernmost point on the earth.

Norway - a kingdom in N Europe, in the W part of the Scandinavian Peninsula.

Olympic Games - the greatest of the games or festivals of ancient Greece, held every four years in the plain of Olympia in Elis, in honor of Zeus; a modern international sports competition, held once every four years.

Ornament - an accessory, article, or detail used to beautify the appearance of something to which it is added or of which it is a part.

Pagan - one of a people or community observing a polytheistic religion, as the ancient Romans and Greeks; a person who is not a Christian, Jew, or Muslim.

Pope - the bishop of Rome as head of the Roman Catholic Church.

President - the highest executive officer of a modern republic, as the Chief Executive of the United States.

Protestant - an adherent of any of those Christian bodies that separated from the Church of Rome during the Reformation, or of any group descended from them.

PVC - polyvinyl chloride; a white, water-insoluble, thermoplastic resin, derived by the polymerization of vinyl chloride: used chiefly for thin coatings, insulation, and piping.

Queen - a female sovereign or monarch.

Reindeer - any of several large deer of the genus *Rangifer,* of northern and arctic regions of Europe, Asia, and North America, both male and female of which have antlers.
Romans - relating to ancient or modern Rome or its people or culture; or relating to the Roman Empire; A native, inhabitant, or citizen of ancient or modern Rome.
Root Ball - Matted roots plus enclosed soil within the pot of a container grown plant
Saint - a person of great holiness, virtue, or benevolence.

Samhain - a festival of the ancient Celts, held around November 1 to celebrate the beginning of winter.

Santa Claus - a benevolent figure of legend, associated with Saint Nicholas, supposed to bring gifts to children on Christmas Eve.

Saturnalia - the festival of Saturn, celebrated in December in ancient Rome as a time of unrestrained merrymaking.

Scandinavia - A region of northern Europe consisting of Norway, Sweden, and Denmark. Finland, Iceland, and the Faeroe Islands.

Scrooge - a miserly curmudgeon in Dickens' Christmas Carol; often any miserly person.

Skyscraper - a relatively tall building of many stories, esp. one for office or commercial use. Architecture. A building of exceptional height completely supported by a framework, as of girders, from which the walls are suspended, as opposed to a building supported by load-bearing walls.

Solstice - either of the two times a year when the sun is at its greatest distance from the celestial equator: about June 21, when the sun reaches its northernmost point on the celestial sphere, or about December 22, when it reaches its southernmost point.

Step Stool - A stool, often with folding steps attached, on which one stands to reach high objects.

Thanksgiving - a national holiday celebrated as a day of feasting and giving thanks for divine favors or goodness, observed on the fourth Thursday of November in the U.S. and in Canada on the second Monday of October.

Thor - the god of thunder, rain, and farming, represented as riding a chariot drawn by goats and wielding the hammer Mjolnir: the defender of the Aesir, destined to kill and be killed by the Midgard Serpent.

Tinsel - a glittering metallic substance, as copper or brass, in thin sheets, used in pieces, strips, threads, etc., to produce a sparkling effect cheaply.

UL - Underwriters' Laboratories (used esp. on labels for electrical appliances approved by this nonprofit safety-testing organization).

United Kingdom - a kingdom in NW Europe, consisting of Great Britain and Northern Ireland: formerly comprising Great Britain and Ireland.

Vikings - One of a seafaring Scandinavian people who raided the coasts of northern and western Europe from the eighth through the tenth century.

Winter - the cold season between autumn and spring in northern latitudes (in the Northern Hemisphere from the winter solstice to the vernal equinox; in the Southern Hemisphere from the summer solstice to the autumnal equinox). The months of December, January, and February in the U.S., and of November, December, and January in Great Britain.

Woolworth, F.W - Franklin Winfield Woolworth, founder of F.W. Woolworth Company. Five and dime store's that were founded in 1878. Headquarters in New York City, New York.

Wreath - a circular band of flowers, foliage, or any ornamental work, for adorning the head or for any decorative purpose; a garland or chaplet.

Yggdrasil - an evergreen ash tree, the three roots of which bind together Asgard, Midgard, and Niflheim.

Yule - Christmas, or the Christmas season.

About the Author

The Author has led an interesting life. He has worked in a variety of fields ranging from Restaurant Management, Licensed Seaman, Educator, Journalist, and, is currently a Registered Nurse working at Elizabethtown Community Hospital, which is nestled in the Adirondack Mountains. Academically he has earned a variety of degrees, which are listed in chronological order: AAA in Mass Media, BA in Communication Arts, AAS in Nursing, and finally a MS in Health Care Administration. He lives with his wife, Virginia, and their two sons, John and Seamus in the Adirondack Mountains in upstate New York. He has published a book titled, Sick Building Syndrome; Fact or Fiction?

Upcoming Projects

Adirondack Cookbook – Due out Summer 2008

This book will provide a wide variety of lip smacking mouth-watering recipes. The recipes come from the restaurants and people from the Adirondack Region in upstate New York. The recipes will range from classics like Irish Soda Bread to Virginia's Mocha Cheesecake. There will be sections on homemade breads, pies, soups, barbeque items, home made pizza, and much more. This book is not designed for the calorie or health conscious. There will be no calorie counts or fat content listed anywhere. This book will be filled with good tasting foods. As an added bonus, a few individual mixed drinks are also included.

www.ingramcontent.com/pod-product-compliance
Ingram Content Group UK Ltd.
Pitfield, Milton Keynes, MK11 3LW, UK
UKHW041924190726
13854UKWH00003B/1430

9 781430 308201